A First Selection of Stories

More short stories for Reciprocal Reading

Chosen by FFT

Published by FFT Education

www.fft.org.uk

The collection of stories and introduction copyright © FFT Education, 2025.

Stories chosen by FFT and introduced by Katie Kielty   ISBN 978-1-911731-99-3

Cover design by Alexander Walker   Printed in the UK by Just Digital

Produced by Oriel Square   First published 2025

We are grateful for permission to include the following stories in this anthology:

'The Wind Ghosts' by Terry Jones from *Fairy Tales* (Puffin, 1987), copyright © Terry Jones 1981, reprinted by permission of the heirs and Estate of Terry Jones.

'Moonflower' by Pippa Goodhart, copyright © Pippa Goodhart 2003, first published in *Give Me Some Space* edited by Kate Agnew (Egmont, 2003), reprinted by permission of the author via Anne Clark Literary Agency.

'The Glass Cupboard' by Terry Jones from *Fairy Tales* (Puffin,1987), copyright © Terry Jones 1981, reprinted by permission of the heirs and Estate of Terry Jones.

'A Sea Find' by Beverley Naidoo, copyright © Beverley Naidoo 2003, commissioned for and first published in *Kid's Night In* (Collins, for Warchild, 2003), reprinted by permission of The Agency (London) Ltd.

'The Amazing Furniture Zoo Park' by Deborah Wright, copyright © Deborah Wright 2003, commissioned for and first published in *Kid's Night In* (Collins, for Warchild, 2003). Copyright holder not traced.

'A Career in Witchcraft' by Kaye Umansky, © Kaye Umansky 1997, first published in *Stacks of Stories* edited by Mary Hoffman (Hodder Children's Books, 1997), reprinted by permission of the author, c/o Rogers, Coleridge & White Ltd, 20 Powis Mews, London W11 1JN.

'Mbango and the Whirlpool' by Lari Don from *Girls, Goddesses & Giants: Tales of Heroines from Around the World* (A&C Black Childrens & Educational, 2013), copyright © Lari Don 2013, reprinted by permission of the publishers, an imprint of Bloomsbury Publishing Plc.

'Komodo Dragon' by Anita Ganeri from *Real Life Dragons and their Stories of Survival*, with illustrations by Jianan Liu (Wayland, 2022), copyright © Wayland 2022, reprinted by permission of Hachette UK Ltd through PLSclear.

Every effort has been made to contact all copyright holders before publication. If notified, the publisher will rectify any errors or omissions at the earliest opportunity.

Contents

Thanks and Acknowledgements

In choosing these texts, there was a whole team involved and so thanks must go to: Eliza Gomez and Catherine Taylor, Lionel Primary School; Becky Taylor, Pye Bank CE Primary School; Lisa Loxton and her class, The Rissington School; and the pupils at Cononley Primary School and Swillington Primary School. Thanks must also go to our younger (but very forthright!) critics: Emily Hicks, Emilia Newby and Jessica Newby.

Introduction

We are incredibly excited to launch this collection of stories, FFT's second anthology. It is intended to be used, primarily, within Reciprocal Reading sessions but is of course adaptable to suit a variety of purposes within your curriculum. This collection is aimed at readers with a reading age of around 7-9 years, whereas our previous anthology, *A Collection of Short Stories*, is aimed at pupils with a reading age of around 9-11 years.

Short stories are a wonderful and often under-used resource to support less confident pupils to have the enjoyment of getting to the end of a story within fewer pages, and in less time, than a novel. Pupils who may be feeling disengaged from reading get the satisfaction of completing a story and enjoying the progression from beginning to middle to end, whilst discussing the story and their views with their peers. Even the deliberate and important 'slowing down' feature of the Reciprocal Reading approach does not delay the completion of a story for too long.

Not all pupils will like every story they read and we must encourage them to have their own views on texts, allowing them to form their own, justified opinions.

Where pupils are less enthusiastic about particular texts, short stories allow for critical opinions to be developed and explored whilst not forcing them to read very long texts they do not enjoy.

For more experienced readers, short stories provide an opportunity to practise reading for meaning. In short stories, no words can be wasted. As a result, it is easier to identify plot developments, see links between moments of significance, and identify how hints and clues are resolved into a clearer meaning. Short stories are satisfying reading and teaching texts because metaphors can be introduced and explored, characters can learn and change, and inferences can be checked, clarified and followed up – all within a few pages.

We hope that by providing you with this resource of short, complete stories, we will support you in moving away from using extracts within teaching. Using sections of texts can often be disorientating for pupils and does not not support the development of a reading-for-pleasure culture; there are lots of gaps in prior knowledge and frustration that an ending is not reached (especially if the full text is not available in school).

By using the four key Reciprocal Reading strategies (predict, clarify, question and summarise) we can bring immediate results in supporting the reader's understanding of details and how these link to the meaning of the text as a whole. For example:

- **Predict**: predictions are easier to link to text clues when the reader is focusing on a relatively limited amount of text.
- **Clarify**: the detailed exploration of vocabulary in context (including metaphorical meanings, word associations, and use of synonyms, morphology and etymology), is more effective when the text is broken down so that misunderstandings are not carried forward and do not adversely affect comprehension across the wider text.
- **Question**: questions are prompted and resolved quickly in shorter texts.
- **Summarise**: summing up the text is easier when events are developed, extended and completed within a few pages.

***

The stories collected here have been chosen not because of any thematic link, but simply as rich examples that will engage and intrigue readers, and reward discussion and investigation. Included is a story of determination and self-belief (*Moonflower*), two modern fairy tales (*The Wind Ghosts* and *The Glass Cupboard*), a real-life account of communication across the globe (*A Sea Find*), an exploration of right and wrong (*The Amazing Furniture Zoo Park*), the everyday meeting the magical (*A Career in Witchcraft*), a retelling of a folk tale (*Mbango and the Whirlpool*) and an account of an extraordinary creature (*Komodo Dragon*).

It is a rich collection that will support better reading for meaning through Reciprocal Reading and other approaches. As someone who enjoys reading a range of text types, I believe comprehension is the key to reading enjoyment – I don't choose to read texts that I don't understand! I hope much discussion, enjoyment and many laughs are generated from the reading of these texts.

Katie Kielty

In Reciprocal Reading training, we emphasise the requirement for the adult to have read the full text prior to teaching, and provide example planning to be edited and used alongside the texts. The stories examine a range of topics and themes, some of which will be more or less suitable and appropriate for your pupils, and therefore we would strongly recommend that the teacher or adult reads the text themselves beforehand.

The Wind Ghosts

By Terry Jones

When the wind is howling round the house and tearing at the clouds, our ears are filled with noise. Chimney pots rattle, doors bang, windows shake. But in-between the blasts, when the wind is still for a moment, you can sometimes hear, very faintly, the pitter-patter footsteps of the ghosts who follow the wind. Here is the story of one such ghost.

Once there were two friends who set off to seek their fortunes. On the first day, they came to a wide river and did not know how to get across. So they walked along the river bank until they came to a little tumble-down hut, where an old woman was sitting making a necklace of bones.

'How do we get across this river, old woman?' they asked.

The old woman kept on threading the bones on the string as if they were beads, and said: 'There are two ways to cross the river. One is free, and one will cost you.'

'How can that be?' asked the two friends.

'Well,' said the old woman, 'one way is to swim across. That's free. The other way is to take the boat that leaves from here at midnight, but that will cost you, for once you step on board you must give the boatman whatever he asks for.'

'I don't want to get wet,' said the first friend, whose name was Jonathan. 'I'll take the boat.'

'Who knows what the boatman might ask for!' said David. 'I'll swim.'

So the two friends agreed to meet the next day on the other side. Then David tied all his belongings in his shirt, put them on his head, and swam across. It was a wide river, and the current took him a long way downstream, but eventually he got to the other side. There he lit a fire and waited until his friend Jonathan arrived.

'Well?' asked David. 'What did the boatman ask for?'

'Oh... he wanted the moon,' said Jonathan.

'So what did you give him?' asked David.

'Oh... I just got out my cup and dipped it in the river and handed it to him so that, when he looked into it, there was the moon, shining up at him.'

***

Well, the two friends went on their way, and on the second day they came to a deep chasm. There they found a little old man, sitting outside a cave.

7

'How do we get across this chasm?' they asked.

'There are two ways,' said the little old man. 'One way will take a minute, the other way will take a month.'

'How can that be?' they asked.

'Well, one way is to walk all round the edge of the chasm, and that will take you a month,' said the little old man. 'The other way is to ask the eagle that lives on this mountain to give you a ride on his back. But if he does, you must answer any question he asks you as you fly over, otherwise he will drop you into the chasm.'

'I'm not going to risk that!' said David. 'I'll walk round the edge, even if it takes a month.'

'I can answer any question,' said Jonathan. 'I'll fly on the eagle's back.'

So the two friends agreed to meet in a month's time. David walked and walked for a whole month, and eventually he reached the spot on the other side of the chasm where they had agreed to meet, and there – sure enough – was his friend Jonathan waiting for him.

'What was the eagle's question?' asked David.

'Oh... he wanted to know where he could always find the summer sun in midwinter,' replied Jonathan.

'What did you tell him?' asked David.

'Oh... I told him to find one blade of grass, for you must know that all plants store the summer sun in their leaves.'

***

So the two friends went on their way until they came to the shore of a sea. There they found an old sailor, so they asked him how they could cross the sea.

'There are two ways,' said the old sailor. 'One way is dangerous, the other way is safe.'

'How can that be?' they asked.

'One way is to sail across on a boat. That will be full of danger, for the sea is deep and there are storms and high waves and sea-monsters. The other way is to go to the wizard of the sea and ask him to get you across by his magic. That is quite safe, but with this warning: you will have to do whatever the wizard of the sea wants first, or else you will never get across at all.'

'I will sail across,' said David, 'for I would rather face the dangers of the sea than put myself in the wizard's hands.'

'I can do whatever the wizard asks me to,' said Jonathan. 'I'll go by magic.'

So Jonathan went to the wizard and swore to do whatever the wizard asked of him.

'There's only one thing you need do for me,' said the wizard, 'and that's not so difficult for someone who can give the moon away and who knows where to find the summer sun in midwinter.'

'What is it I must do?' asked Jonathan.

'You must catch the wind,' said the wizard. And just then a breeze blew across the shore, and Jonathan set off after it.

Meanwhile David had built himself a boat. He spread his sail, and the wind blew him across the ocean. Sometimes the wind blew up a storm, and sometimes it blew him the wrong way, and he fought with the rain and the cold and the sea-monsters, but at length he got to the other side. There he built a windmill, and the wind turned the sails of the mill, and he became a miller. He never grew rich, but he was never poor, and – for all I know – he was happy enough.

Jonathan, however, never *was* able to catch the wind, and to this day he chases after it, and in between the blasts of a storm you may hear the pitter-patter of his footsteps. He cannot stop, and he cannot catch it, for he is now a wind ghost. And yet – for all I know – he *too* is happy enough... in his way.

Moonflower

By Pippa Goodhart

Meera's body sat at the table in the classroom with the other children, but her mind was floating up into the sky outside. She chewed on her pen and gazed out of the window at the moon shining pale in the morning sky. It looked, thought Meera, like a chapati, round and dimpled. If you didn't know better, you'd think that the moon was as flat as a chapati too. Things weren't always as they seemed.

'Perhaps Meera can tell us?' Mrs Johnson's sharp voice made Meera jump.

'Moonbeaming again, Meera? Or can you tell us what conditions a plant needs in order to grow?'

'Er ...' Meera looked to her twin, sitting two tables away, but Seema wasn't offering any help. Meera thought about the pots growing herbs on the windowsill at home. Mum sometimes got her to water them.

'They need water,' said Meera.

'Good,' said Mrs Johnson. 'What else?'

'Um, I suppose they need soil too, or they'd fall over.'

'Water and soil and ...?' Every face in the classroom was looking at her now, and Meera's brain went blank. She blushed and looked away. Mrs Johnson sighed. Meera knew she was thinking, 'I never have this trouble with Seema'. Some people said it out loud, but Meera knew that lots more people thought it.

Meera and Seema were the same on the outside but, on the inside, one was a good girl and the other was 'difficult'. Seema was the good girl. She did what she was told, promptly and neatly and well. Meera didn't. Meera found the conversations she could have in her own mind were nearly always more interesting than what teachers and parents and even friends told her. So she moonbeamed, escaping into her mind and away from the classroom, or kitchen, or wherever she was at the time. It made teachers cross. Mrs Johnson scowled.

'Can anybody help Meera with the answer?' Yes, they all could. Arms shot up all around.

'Sunlight. Plants need sunlight!'

'That's right,' said Mrs Johnson. 'And now I'm going to let you all have a go at growing a plant. We'll have a little competition to see who can grow the tallest sunflower, and we'll experiment by giving each of the plants slightly different conditions to see exactly what suits them best.'

Mrs Johnson looked down her nose at Meera, then smiled at the rest of the class. 'I expect that Meera will grow hers without giving it any sunlight at all!' They all laughed, all looking at Meera, but this time Meera tossed her dark plait over her shoulder, crossed her arms and glared back.

'As a matter of fact,' she said, 'I will!'

'Oh, indeed?' said Mrs Johnson. 'And do you think you have a chance of winning?'

'I might!' said Meera. Seema rolled her eyes to show what she thought of that, and she laughed with the others.

***

Mrs Johnson gave out the seeds next morning. Seema had brought some of Gran's fruitcake to mix with soil for hers. 'It should make the seeds grow fast,' she told Meera. 'Remember how Gran said her cake is nourishing with all those raisins in it? Some of the boys are watering theirs with apple juice and orange juice. And Katie's putting a bit of chocolate near hers because she thinks the smell will make the plant want to grow out of the soil to reach it. That'd work on me! Have you decided what to do with yours yet, Meera?'

'I told you yesterday,' said Meera. 'I'm growing mine without sunlight.'

'Not really? But it won't grow, you know, not without any light. Mrs Johnson said so.'

'I never said it wasn't going to have any light,' said Meera. Then she turned away and wouldn't say any more. But she could feel Seema watching her as she put soil into the plastic flowerpot, pushed in a slim, stripy seed, and watered it from a jam-jar. Then she covered the pot with a bag she'd made out of black paper to keep it dark.

'Line the pots up on the windowsill,' said Mrs Johnson. 'Make sure your name is clearly marked.'

'But mine mustn't have any sunlight,' said Meera.

'Well, if you're going to insist on this silliness, then you'd better put yours into the stock-cupboard. But I think we all know what the result of this is going to be,' sighed Mrs Johnson.

'Can I take it with me when it's going-home time, please?' asked Meera.

'Whatever for?'

'Part of my experiment,' said Meera.

'Oh, if you must, Meera,' said Mrs Johnson.

***

Seema tried to walk home beside Meera.

'Why are you taking your pot home?' she asked. 'You're being really stupid, you know. Everybody thinks so. Why don't you grow it properly in the light like everybody else? That's what Mrs Johnson wants you to do.'

But Meera marched on, holding her covered pot in front of her, and she didn't answer.

***

Meera and Seema went to bed at their normal time, but Meera didn't go to sleep. She lay on top of her hairbrush to make sure she was too uncomfortable for that. She waited and listened to the sounds of Seema's breathing becoming slow and sleepy. She heard her parents going to bed, heard her little brother going downstairs for a glass of water, and then stillness, marked by the tick-tock of the clock on her bedside table. Meera watched the curtains and, finally, just after midnight, they began to glow with light as the moonshine reached them.

Silently, Meera pushed back her covers and then the curtains. She took the black cover off her seed in a pot and sat the pot on the windowsill in a stream of silvery moonlight.

'There's your light, little seed,' she whispered. 'Now get growing and show Seema and the others that you can beat them all!'

She knelt at the window, her head propped on her hands, and she gazed out at the big silvery-blue moon and thought of the men who had stood on the moon and bounced around and stuck in a flag and then gone home. She thought to herself, I bet their teachers told them it was stupid to think they could ever stand on the moon.

The moon moved across the sky as Meera watched and thought. When the moonlight left the window, Meera shaded her pot and got back into bed, but her mind kept thinking about what seemed impossible but might just be possible as she warmed to sleep.

**

Next morning the children looked at the bare soil in their pots.

'It'll be a few days before there's anything to see,' said Mrs Johnson. Yet that evening, when Meera uncovered her pot in the moonlight, there was already something green poking through the soil in her pot. Meera threw her plait over her shoulder and smiled as she put it in the moonlight once more.

Over the next few nights, Meera watched for moonlight and uncovered her growing young plant to moonbathe in the light each night.

'Why do you keep yawning?' asked Seema at school. 'Mrs Johnson's been giving you funny looks.' But Meera didn't tell. Night after night, she kept herself awake while Seema slept and watched as her little plant grew, a bit like somebody sitting up in bed, stretching sleepy arms, and turning to see the moonlight coming in through the window. The green spike of life grew upward, spreading wide two fresh green leaves.

Meera knew that the other children were muttering things and laughing at her at school, but she didn't care. She found a bamboo cane in the garden shed and pushed that into the soil and carefully tied her plant to it with soft wool to try and keep it strong and tall. Seema watched as the black paper hood over the pot in their bedroom was replaced by taller and taller hoods. She didn't ask Meera questions about it any more. And she'd given up watering her own seed in a pot after it began to go fluffy with mould. 'Mine's not going to work,' she told Meera.

Then, one moonlight night, Meera's plant bloomed into flower. It unfurled a broad speckled silver-gold circle fringed with narrow silvery-white petals.

'I'm taking it to school today,' Meera told Seema next morning. 'Would you like to see it before the others?' Seema nodded. So, with their bedroom curtains holding back the sunlight, Meera took the hood off her plant.

'Oh!' said Seema, and her hands fluttered to her mouth. Then she looked at Meera. 'But it isn't a sunflower, is it?'

'No,' said Meera. 'It's a moonflower, grown in moonlight. That's why it's different.'

Seema touched the flower very gently. 'It's beautiful,' she said.

Seema carried Meera's bag so that Meera could carry the tall plant to school. Meera put the pot on her table and put her hand up.

'Meera, yes?' said Mrs Johnson.

'My plant's got a flower,' said Meera. Everyone went quiet and turned to look at her.

'Already?' said Mrs Johnson, glancing at the row of pots on the windowsill where a few tiny shoots were showing but not anywhere near big enough to flower. 'That's rather surprising when your plant hasn't had any sunlight to help it grow.'

There were a few tittering laughs around the class.

'It's had moonlight,' said Meera.

'Oh,' said Mrs Johnson, 'I see. Well, perhaps you'd better show it to us.'

So Meera lifted the black hood from her plant and there were gasps and then silence all around as, for just a moment or two, the silver-white flower shone luminously, before its brightness dulled and the flower began to wilt as they watched. Nobody said anything, then Mrs Johnson snorted a kind of laugh.

'Well, I must admit that I've never seen anything quite like that before, Meera, but I am quite sure no plant can grow without sunlight. You look in any book on the subject and you'll see that I'm right.'

'Books don't know everything,' said Meera. Mrs Johnson went pink.

'They know a great deal more than any cheeky little girl does! And I feel quite sure that if I look in a book of garden weeds, I shall find a fast-growing, scraggly plant with a big grey flower, and that you, Meera, have planted one of those in your pot and tried to trick us all. I don't believe for a moment that you've been up catching the moonlight and growing your seed that way! You'd better throw that horrid plant in the bin!'

The plant had lost its beauty as Mrs Johnson talked, wilting in the sunlight and the scorn, and Meera seemed to have wilted too. But suddenly Seema was on her feet.

'You're wrong, Mrs Johnson,' she said. 'Meera has done it properly. I've seen her in the night when she thought I was asleep. It's a real moonflower, grown from the seed you gave her and it should win the prize!' Mrs Johnson blinked rapidly.

'The prize is for the tallest sunflower, Seema. It is not for moonflowers. Now, Meera, throw that thing away and then I want you all to take out your maths books.'

The moonflower plant had wizened as they watched, and its petals had fallen. Meera slowly tipped it, pot and plant, into the bin. Then she glanced at Mrs Johnson who was busy writing on the board. Meera bent down and quickly took something back out of the bin; something that she held tight in a fist. She sat down beside Seema. As the others took out their maths books, Meera uncurled her fist to show Seema four slim, stripy silver things in a palm. 'Seeds,' she said.

'Can I help with them?' whispered Seema.

Mrs Johnson frowned. 'I want quiet, please!'

But Seema took no notice. She was looking at Meera who smiled and nodded, 'We'll grow them together.'

Then they both tossed back their plaits and gazed out of the window and wondered about the moon and space and whatever was beyond, while Mrs Johnson talked about fractions.

The Glass Cupboard

by Terry Jones

There was once a cupboard that was made entirely of glass so you could see right into it and right through it. Now, although this cupboard always appeared to be empty, you could always take out whatever you wanted. If you wanted a cool drink, for example, you just opened the cupboard and took one out. Or if you wanted a new pair of shoes, you could always take a pair out of the glass cupboard. Even if you wanted a bag of gold, you just opened up the glass cupboard and took out a bag of gold. The only thing you had to remember was that, whenever you took something *out* of the glass cupboard, you had to put something else back *in*, although nobody quite knew why.

Naturally such a valuable thing as the glass cupboard belonged to a rich and powerful King.

One day, the King had to go on a long journey, and while he was gone some thieves broke into the palace and stole the glass cupboard.

'Now we can have anything we want,' they said.

One of the robbers said: 'I want a large bag of gold,' and he opened the glass cupboard and took out a large bag of gold.

Then the second robber said: 'I want two large bags of gold,' and he opened the glass cupboard and took out two large bags of gold.

Then the chief of the robbers said: 'I want three of the biggest bags of gold you've ever seen!' and he opened the glass cupboard and took out three of the biggest bags of gold you've ever seen.

'Hooray!' they said. 'Now we can take out as much gold as we like!'

Well, those three robbers stayed up the whole night, taking bag after bag of gold out of the glass cupboard. But not one of them put anything back in.

In the morning, the chief of the robbers said: 'Soon we shall be the richest three men in the world. But let us go to sleep now, and we can take out more gold tonight.'

So they lay down to sleep. But the first robber could not sleep. He kept thinking: 'If I went to the glass cupboard just *once* more, I'd be even richer than I am now.' So he got up, and went to the cupboard, and took out yet another bag of gold, and then went back to bed.

And the second robber could not sleep either. He kept thinking: 'If I went to the glass cupboard and took out two more bags of gold, I'd be even richer than the others.' So he got up, and went to the cupboard, and took out two more bags of gold, and then went back to bed.

Meanwhile the chief of the robbers could not sleep either. He kept thinking: 'If I went to the glass cupboard and took out three more bags of gold, I'd be the richest of all.' So he got up, and went to the cupboard, and took out three more bags of gold, and then went back to bed.

And then the first robber said to himself: 'What am I doing, lying here sleeping, when I could be getting richer?' So he got up, and started taking more and more bags of gold out of the cupboard.

The second robber heard him and thought: 'What am I doing, lying here sleeping, when he's getting richer than me?' So he got up and joined his companion.

And then the chief of the robbers got up too. 'I can't lie here sleeping,' he said, 'while the other two are both getting richer than me.' So he got up and soon all three were hard at it, taking more and more bags of gold out of the cupboard.

And all that day and all that night not one of them dared to stop for fear that one of his companions would get richer than him. And they carried on all the next day and all the next night. They didn't stop to rest, and they didn't stop to eat, and they didn't even stop to drink. They kept taking out those bags of gold faster and faster and more and more until, at length, they grew faint with lack of sleep and food and drink, but still they did not dare to stop.

All that week and all the next week, and all that month and all that winter, they kept at it, until the chief of the robbers could bear it no longer, and he picked up a hammer and smashed the glass cupboard into a million pieces, and they all three gave a great cry and fell down dead on top of the huge mountain of gold they had taken out of the glass cupboard.

***

Sometime later the King returned home, and his servants threw themselves on their knees before him, and said: 'Forgive us, Your Majesty, but three wicked robbers have stolen the glass cupboard!'

The King ordered his servants to search the length and breadth of the land. When they found what was left of the glass cupboard, and the three robbers lying dead, they filled sixty great carts with all the gold and took it back to the King. And when the King heard that the glass cupboard was smashed into a million pieces and that the three thieves were dead, he shook his head and said: 'If those thieves had always put something back into the cupboard for every bag of gold they had taken out, they would be alive to this day.' And he ordered his servants to collect all the pieces of the glass cupboard and to melt them down and make them into a globe with all the countries of the world upon it, to remind himself, and others, that the earth is as fragile as that glass cupboard.

A Sea Find

by Beverley Naidoo

Scarves and caps
tightly wrapped,
we pace along the beach
one blue-rimmed Christmas Day.
Eyes tracing wet patterns on the sand
touch something glistening green.
'Some people!
Don't care do they?
Throw their litter anywhere!'
A bottle deep-sea green
lies beside a clump of seaweed.

'It could be dangerous and—'
'Hey look! It's corked!
Something's inside!'
'Open it!'
'Go on!'
Through the murky glass
a piece of paper
suggests a small mystery.
We struggle with the cork
till, popping through,
a child's words
speak out
in French!
MON NOM EST KATIA
J'ai 5 ans
Écrivez-moi s'il vous plaît!
Underneath
in neat letters
an address across the ocean!
Beside us
the waves break steadily, calmly.

But looking out as far as the eye can see,
remembering night-splintering storms,
we wonder and marvel
at this glassy capsule
which has bobbed safely to our shore.

The story behind this poem

This really happened! We were walking along the beach on our first Christmas Day in Bournemouth when we stumbled on a mucky green bottle. It was chance that one of us spotted the paper inside. The message in French was easy to translate. *My name is Katia. I am 5 years old. Write to me please!* Underneath was an address of an infant school in Plouescat. I wrote it down in my writer's notebook. At home we checked our map. Plouescat was at the far end of Brittany, the bit that juts out into the Atlantic Ocean like a dog's nose. Had the bottle travelled all that way?

Our daughter Maya, just ten, sent a postcard. I helped her write it in French. A couple of weeks later, a letter arrived in a young child's handwriting. It was from Katia and '*Les Chicolodenns de Plouescat*'. It began '*Bonjour Famille Naidoo*' and ended with the Breton greeting '*Kenaro*'. The children sent us drawings and wanted to know about our family. Did we keep dogs, cats, calves, pigs or chickens? Maya replied and the correspondence took off. It was a great way to begin learning French. The class had a wonderfully imaginative teacher. Mlle Evelyne le Guern sent letters and books made by the children, photographs, postcards, newspaper cuttings and all sorts of memorabilia. Maya, in turn, wrote letters and illustrated little books about us.

Katia and her friends moved on and their teacher introduced us to her next class. When she retired to an even more remote part of

Brittany, she continued to write and send gifts at Christmas to Maya with delicious Breton biscuits for the family. Maya carried on learning French. During her A levels she visited Mlle le Guern who, in turn, made her first trip over the Channel to visit us. She told us about her childhood during the war under Nazi occupation. We told her about South Africa under apartheid. Her family's history is deeply Breton. Ours is full of journeys across oceans and continents. Maya is grown-up now, speaks French, loves learning new languages and she and I have written our first book together – with a sea theme! Mlle le Guern and I have grey hairs. But our family friendship and sharing of stories, that began with a child's letter in a bottle, live on.

The Amazing Furniture Zoo Park

by Deborah Wright

Tristan woke up on the morning of his seventh birthday feeling rather miserable. He glanced down at the bottom of his bed. It was unlikely that his parents had bought him any presents, since they'd forgotten for the last seven years running, but he could always hope.

His heart leapt. There *was* something at the bottom of his bed. It looked like a card.

It was made out of a folded piece of toilet paper. Tristan opened it up and sighed. Inside, it said: HAPPY BIRTHDAY TOM! They hadn't even managed to get his name right.

As you might have guessed by now, Tristan's parents weren't exactly wonderful people.

The trouble was, they were both much too much in love with money to care about their only son. They both worked all of the day and most of the night in a large bank in London. They were very stingy when it came to pocket money; Tristan only got one pence a week and if he was bad, it often went into minus numbers, which was charged at a rate of twenty-five per cent interest.

Tristan got dressed and went downstairs, hoping he might, just might, have *one* tiny little present.

'Presents!' his mother cried. She was standing behind an ironing board, frantically rubbing her iron over some crumpled fifty-pound notes to make them smooth and crisp. 'I can't talk now, I'm too busy! Ask your father.'

'Presents!' his father cried. He was standing in the kitchen, lightly grilling a five-pound note. His father loved money so much he liked to eat it; he said it tasted much nicer than toast. 'Now look what you've made me do!' he cried as the note burst into flames. 'You distracted me! Your pocket money this month is now minus fifty-seven pounds, and 3.0005000 pence!'

'Thanks,' said Tristan sullenly. 'Oh, and by the way,' he added, 'my name is Tristan. Not Tom. You got my birthday card wrong.'

'That's another fifty pence off for being cheeky,' his father blustered.

'*Dad, that's not fair*!' Tristan cried.

'Shut up!' said his mother, storming into the kitchen. 'Your father and I are late for work. Now you can do something useful and spend the day reading the *Financial Times* and deciding which shares you'd buy – if you ever manage to earn any money.'

As his parents zoomed off to work, Tristan trudged up to his bedroom and sat by the window, feeling rather miserable. The clouds were grey and grumpy and it was just starting to rain. It wasn't going to be much of a fun day, just sitting and watching the rain form watery spiders' webs across the glass.

To cheer himself up, Tristan sank into his favourite fantasy daydream. He was a superhero, battling against villains and saving people's lives (especially beautiful young girls). He was just about to do battle with an alien spaceship when—

—suddenly the doorbell rang. Tristan's heart leapt. But it sank pretty quickly when he glanced down and saw who it was: his mad Uncle Max.

Tristan didn't like his Uncle Max very much. He was old and had a hoary grey beard and smelt of Bovril and, most of all, he was completely bonkers. Unfortunately, before

Tristan could hide, his uncle looked up and spotted him.

'AHA!' he shouted. 'DON'T TRY TO HIDE, YOU IMPUDENT BOY! I'M COMING UP TO GET YOU!'

And then his uncle did something that made Tristan gawp in amazement. He opened up his large green umbrella and sailed up to the window.

'Come on, birthday boy,' he said, grabbing hold of Tristan with one hand whilst hanging on to the extraordinary umbrella with the other. 'We're going out for the day. We're going to the zoo! Come on, Umbrella!'

'All right, all right,' a female voice came from nowhere.

When Tristan looked down, he felt his stomach lurch. He closed his eyes and hung on tightly as they swung into a large froth of cloud.

Well, he thought to himself, *this is all pretty strange. Still, it is much more fun than staying at home and reading about shares...*

When he opened his eyes, the clouds had parted and they were sailing to the ground. It was then that Tristan realised this was no ordinary zoo. There was a large pink neon sign outside that blazed: MAD UNCLE MAX'S AMAZING FURNITURE ZOO PARK.

'*Furniture* zoo park?' Tristan asked. 'Isn't that a bit weird?'

'You must be weird to think it's weird,' said Uncle Max. 'Now come on, you impudent boy. We don't have to queue, since I own the zoo. We can go right on in.'

He folded his umbrella, ignoring her squeak-shrieks of protest and tucked her under his arm.

Inside the zoo, they walked up to the first cage. It was filled with tall green trees and bushes. A few large slabs of pink meat, oozing juice, were lying on the grass. There were signs plastered all over the cages saying: DANGER! DO NOT TOUCH THE FENCE! YOU MAY BE BITTEN!

A crowd had gathered round. People were pointing and whispering nervously. Tristan frowned.

'What's in it?' he asked his uncle.

'Can't you see?' his uncle whispered, pointing.

Yes, he could see *something*... behind those trees... a flash of pink...

All of a sudden a large pink flowery sofa jumped out from behind the trees. It munched some grass, growling uneasily at the crowds.

Tristan started to laugh, but his uncle gave him a stern look, so he quickly shut up. 'Look,' said his uncle.

Tristan looked. Something blue was flashing behind the trees...

Another sofa!

This one was blue with white stripes. It seemed to be creeping up behind the pink sofa...

The pink sofa hadn't noticed...

'Ooh,' the crowd gasped. A little boy started to cling to his father's leg and whimper in terror. Even Tristan couldn't help feeling a little afraid. The sofa *did* look fierce, pausing and sniffing the wind, seeming to sense that it was being watched.

'Look out,' Tristan whispered, his heart beating.

Crash! The blue sofa pounced on to the pink one. The pink one fell on its side, looking surprised and dazed. The blue one knocked it again, buffeting it with big, hard blows.

'Fight! Fight! Fight!' Uncle Max cried in excitement, roaring with laughter as the two sofas started to tussle with each other, rolling over and over in the grass.

'What's that!?' Tristan cried, seeing something yellow and fluffy on the grass.

Then he realised it was stuffing. There was a large gash in the side of the pink sofa and the stuffing was pouring out.

'My sofas!' Uncle Max rattled the cage. 'Don't let them kill each other!'

A zoo keeper quickly jumped up and hosed a stream of water on to them. They leapt apart, sopping wet, growling rather grumpily. The crowds moved on, looking nervous.

Tristan turned to his uncle. 'That was amazing!' he cried. 'But are they alive? Or are they robots?'

'Robots! Of course not! Just because you can move around, do people ask you if you're a robot? No they don't, you rude child! Listen, all furniture is alive. The furniture sitting back in your home right now is alive.'

'What?' Tristan really thought that Uncle Max had gone completely and utterly bonkers now; his brain cells had clearly fallen out in the night and were lying at home on his pillow. 'Are you trying to say,' Tristan asked, 'that my bed and the table and the TV and the mixer in the kitchen and the oven and... and... all those things are alive?'

'Exactly. They're very crafty creatures. They're so clever that they can sit still all day without moving. But the next time you're home, take a very close look at your sofa or TV – you'll see just a very slight movement. They have to move a millimetre or so because they're breathing.'

'Oh really?' said Tristan doubtfully. Because deep down inside he still didn't quite believe him. The idea was simply preposterous. But then again, so was a green umbrella that flew and talked.

'Now come on, on we go – we have to go to the exotic house now.'

As they left, Tristan had a funny feeling that something was wrong. But his uncle was walking ahead at such a brisk pace that Tristan ignored his heart and hurried on.

***

They continued their tour of the zoo and saw all kinds of weird and wonderful creatures. They had photographs taken with cushions on their laps and curtains draped round their shoulders (which was quite difficult when the curtains kept hissing and slithering off).

'Here,' said his uncle, passing him a pink curtain with a slightly shy smile, 'you can keep one to take home. Don't forget to feed it, mind. It needs three large curtain hooks a day.'

'Er, thanks,' said Tristan, draping it over his arm. It wasn't quite the pet he'd always dreamed of, but he was touched by his uncle's kindness.

They saw food mixers in glass cages playfully throwing liquidised fruit over each other. Once, Tristan even glanced up and saw knives and forks flying overhead, migrating to countries where they would be used to eat warmer foods.

They came to an enclosure with a large turquoise pool. A keeper held out a pair of fish and then – *whoosh!* – a pair of Hoovers came flying up out of the water, snapping up the fish in their metal jaws. A few seconds later, their dust bags were filled with silvery bones and they vroom-vroomed hungrily for more.

Lastly, they came to a cage filled with Walkmans and hi-fis. A keeper was trying to remove the hi-fis' aerials, wincing as they emitted fuzzy little squeals of pain.

'They're being neutered,' Uncle Max explained. 'They breed like rabbits otherwise!'

'Is it safe to put Walkmans and hi-fis together?' Tristan asked nervously. 'Don't they fight each other?'

'Don't be stupid,' said his uncle. 'Everyone knows that Walkmans grow up to be radios – what do they teach you in school these days?'

Tristan noticed that batteries kept falling out of the Walkmans and thudding to the floor.

'Won't they go flat?' he asked.

'Run flat? As I've told you before, they're not robots, they're alive. No, it's poo!'

'Poo?' Tristan asked in disbelief. 'Poo?'

'People are very polite in England so they call them batteries. Unfortunately, they've got diarrhoea at the moment, because they've been playing too many Westlife albums – enough to make anyone feel ill, I should think. Ah,' he checked his watch. 'Goodness me, how the day has flown. Time to go home I think...'

He was about to send Tristan off with a pat on the head and a jar of Bovril, when he heard a sudden growling noise behind him.

'LOOK OUT!' Tristan cried.

But it was too late. His uncle turned in bewilderment as the blue and white striped sofa that had been hovering in the shadows behind them, finally pounced.

Tristan gasped as it flung its cushions against his uncle's head, battering him to the ground. *It must have escaped from its cage,* he realised. *Oh dear God, I knew there was something wrong; the cage wasn't locked properly, if only I'd said something.*

His uncle had now disappeared under the sofa, which was making guzzling sounds. What could he do? What could he do?

'Here boy, here,' Tristan tried to whistle, but the sofa seemed too busy enjoying gobbling up his uncle.

Then, as he gazed down at his arm, inspiration struck. He picked up the pink curtain and waved it temptingly.

The sofa paused and let out an *mmmmmmm-that-looks-yummy* noise. Then he lunged at the curtain.

Tristan started to run, waving the curtain (the poor thing was shrieking in terror) as the sofa came after him in hot pursuit. He felt its flowery hem snapping at his heels and his heart started to hammer. He was nearly there, nearly there.

He rounded the corner – and *wham!* – the waiting keepers held open the cage door. Tristan darted aside and the sofa went skidding back into its cage. The keepers burst into a round of applause. One of them took the whimpering curtain away, gently stroking it better.

'Well, thank goodness for my brilliant nephew!' his uncle cried, staggering to his feet and slapping a meaty hand on Tristan's shoulder. 'You, my dear boy, are a real hero.'

Though Tristan had always fantasised about fighting aliens rather than sofas, he couldn't help a glow of pride sweeping over him. He looked up at his uncle and decided that, despite the fact that he was old and had a hoary grey beard and was totally bonkers, he really rather liked him.

Uncle Max looked down at Tristan and smiled back.

'You can come back anytime to the zoo. I'll give you a season ticket. Then, whenever you're bored, just think of me and I'll pop up with the umbrella.'

'Thanks,' said Tristan gratefully. 'I'd like that very much.'

***

Back home, Tristan felt rather happy. It had been the best birthday he'd had in a long time, even if it had been rather strange.

He was so tired after so much excitement that he collapsed on to the sofa and fell into a deep sleep. When he woke up several hours later, the day's adventures suddenly flashed before him. He sat up and gazed around the living room in awe. Could the furniture really be alive?

Tristan jiggled up and down on the sofa. Nothing happened. He tiptoed up to the TV and tweaked the aerial. Nothing happened.

I'm being stupid, thought Tristan. *Soon people will be calling me Mad Nephew Tristan. Of course it isn't alive. This is the real world and the furniture zoo was just a dream...*

And then he heard a noise. It came from the sofa, and it seemed as though the sofa was reminding him of what the reality was...

It sounded – if he listened very hard – like a long, low, snarling growl...

Tristan smiled wickedly and sat down, waiting for his parents to come home.

A Career in Witchcraft

by Kaye Umansky

'Got anythin' on a career in witchcraft?'

Mr Smike gave a heavy sigh. He was in the middle of one of his favourite tasks – noting down the names of all the people who owed library fines. He could have done without the interruption.

He set down his pen with an irritable click and peered over the desk.

'What?' he said.

"I said, got anythin' on a career in witchcraft? Please?'

The speaker was a small girl, aged about sevenish, eightish, nineish, who cared? She stared solemnly up at him through a pair of owlish glasses. She wore a black woolly dress and a cardboard witch hat decorated with clumsily cut out moons and stars. A plastic bin liner, pinned with safety pins, hung from her shoulders. She was clutching a small broomstick.

For a brief moment, Mr Smike was taken aback. Then, he remembered. Of course. Tonight was October the thirty-first – Hallowe'en. The child was obviously all dressed up to go Trick Or Treating – an activity of which he heartily disapproved. Gangs of giggling vampires, skeletons, ghosts and masked monsters would be tramping the streets until all hours of the night, he supposed, leaning on doorbells and waving plastic bags under people's noses and demanding chocolate with menaces. Well, as far as Mr Smike was concerned, they could forget it. There would be no sweets, pennies or tangerines forthcoming from *him*. Any child unwise enough to come calling at *his* house tonight would get nothing but a stiff lecture.

'Careers over in the corner,' said Mr Smike, shortly.

'Which corner? There's four,' said the small girl.

'That one.' He jerked his head. 'And you can leave that stick here,' he ordered severely. 'I don't want bits of twig scattered all over the floor.'

For a split second, the small girl looked mutinous. Then, she gave a little nod and carefully propped her broomstick against the desk before heading off between the book racks. Mr Smike watched her, noting with disapproval that her socks had fallen down.

Mr Smike wasn't fond of children. Noisy, ill-mannered little brats with their shrill little voices and grubby little hands. The less he had to do with them, the better. Normally he would be over in the reference section of the main library, but Mrs Jaunty, the children's librarian, had rung in sick and there was nobody else to fill in.

He cast a jaundiced eye over the place. Picture books, hah! Cushions, jigsaw puzzles, mobiles, posters, murals, double hah! This wasn't a proper library. It didn't have QUIET notices all over the place. There wasn't even a box marked FINES. Great hordes of school children had been in and out all day, putting their unwashed fingers all over the books. The place had been chock-a-block with chattering mums pushing buggies full of snotty-nosed toddlers who waddled around the place getting underfoot. They treated the place like a hotel. It wasn't his kind of library at all.

Oh well. Thankfully, it was nearly closing time. With a bit of luck, that Jaunty creature would be back tomorrow, dispensing books and smiles and organising poetry competitions and story telling sessions and whatever else the silly woman did to keep the little monsters happy.

Mr Smike picked up his pen and returned to his list. Mrs C. Randall – two books, three weeks overdue at twenty pence a day, that would be eight pounds forty. Wayne Geeke, four books out on motorbike maintenance, should have been returned a month ago, that would be twenty two pounds forty and serve the cocky young lout right for having such an anti-social hobby. Old Albert Bedlam, the large print version of *Managing On A Low Income*, a full ten days overdue. Two pounds exactly. That'd make a tidy hole in his pension. J. Sugden, six books out, two weeks late, oh, excellent, excellent! Now let's see, that would be...

'There isn't one.'

The small girl was back again, ogling him over the desk with her magnified eyes which were, he noticed, a kind of fishy green.

'Isn't what?' snapped Mr Smike.

'A *Career in Witchcraft* book. There's nursin' and hairdressin' an' ballet dancin' an' lawyerin' an' bein' a TV presenter an' that, but nothin' on witchcraft.'

'In that case,' said Mr Smike, with great satisfaction, 'I can't help you, can I?'

There was a little pause. Mr Smike went back to his list, hoping that the annoying child would give up and go away.

'Where's the lady?' asked the small girl, standing her ground.

'At home, sick,' Mr Smike told her, with even greater satisfaction.

'The lady'd help me. She's nice. She found me lots of useful stuff. Spells and that. That's how I got my broomstick goin'. Couldn't get it to budge until she helped me find the right book. Goes like the clappers now.'

She reached out and gave the propped up broomstick a satisfied little pat.

'Indeed,' muttered Mr Smike, not looking up.

'Oh, yes. She got me a great book on *Herbs What Can Heal*. I can get rid of warts now. And boils. You got any warts or boils need fixin'?'

'No.' Mr Smike glanced pointedly at the library clock. Only another two minutes, then he could throw out this revolting child and never again have to endure her bizarre fantasies.

'Got anythin' new in on toads?' persisted his tormentor.

'No.'

'Bats?'

'No.'

'Anythin' that'll tell me where to get hold of an eye of a newt?'

'Little girl.' Mr Smike spoke wearily. He leaned forward and frowned down at her, tapping his pen. 'Little girl. Don't you think this obsession with witchcraft is a little unhealthy? What does your mother say?'

'Oh, she's all for it.' The small girl placed her elbows on the desk in what Mr Smike considered to be an over-familiar way. 'Well, she would be, wouldn't she? Bein' one herself an' that.'

'I beg your pardon?'

'Ma. She's a witch.'

'Oh, I *see!* And I suppose she's back in the cave, mixing up a brew?' enquired Mr Smike with cold sarcasm.

'Well, it's not a cave,' the small girl informed him seriously. 'This isn't the dark ages, you know. It's a proper house. But you're right about the brew. She's getting it ready for tonight's party. All me aunties are round helpin', an' cacklin' so loud I can't do me homework. Ma said to come along here an' look up stuff for meself in the library. She's trainin' me up, but she reckons you learn better if you look up stuff for yourself. An' that's what I'm doin'.'

'It's a great pity she hasn't trained you up not to tell lies, young lady,' said Mr Smike nastily. 'There are no such things as witches.' He pointed to the clock. 'See that? One minute to closing time. I suggest you remove your elbows from my desk, choose yourself a suitable book and then run along home.'

'I don't tell lies,' objected the small girl. Her green eyes flashed. 'An' there *are* such things as witches!' she added, with spirit. 'I know, 'cos I'm gonna be one. So there.'

'One minute,' repeated Mr Smike through gritted teeth. The small girl stared at him.

'You don't believe me, do you?' she said.

'I most certainly do not believe you,' replied Mr Smike grimly. 'I've never *heard* such twaddle. Too much television, that's your trouble.'

'We haven't got a television. Ma's got a crystal ball, but I'm not allowed to use it. Except on Saturday mornin's when she's havin' a lie in.'

Mr Smike had had enough of all this. He wagged a warning finger under the small girl's nose.

'Young lady,' he said. His voice was so sharp, you could have sliced cucumber with it. 'This is not funny. You can take a joke too far. Some people may find your flights of fancy amusing, but I am not one of them.'

There was a short silence. The small girl continued to stare at him. The clock ticked. Then:

'So you don't have anythin' on a career in witchcraft, then?'

'No!' shouted Mr Smike. 'I do not! You have no business wandering in here pestering busy adults with your ridiculous requests. You are a silly little girl with a head full of rubbish. And you can tell your mother I said so.'

The small girl went very red. There was another short silence. Then:

'I could turn you into a frog, I could,' she muttered with a scowl. And she turned abruptly on her heel and set off back down the racks.

***

Mr Smike felt pleased with himself. He had told her, oh yes indeed. You had to be firm with these cheeky young things. Briskly, he gathered up his papers, slipped them into his briefcase and clipped his pen into his breast pocket. He would finish the list at home. It would be something to look forward to after supper. Then, if there was time, he would write another of his complaining letters to the local paper. (Mr Smike wrote a lot of complaining letters to newspapers. It was a kind of hobby. He wrote about the state of the drains, the surliness of dustmen, the laziness of the unemployed and the trouble with Youth Today. If the paper didn't publish them, he wrote and complained about *that*.)

He opened a drawer, took out the library key in readiness and waited, eyes on the clock, tapping his foot impatiently and willing it to move on. Thirty seconds to go.

'I'll take this one,' said the small girl, appearing again and slamming a book under his nose. '*Baba Yaga*. It's got my great, great, great, great, great-gran in it. She was Russian, you know,' she added, with a certain amount of defiant pride.

'Ticket,' said Mr Smike coldly, snapping his fingers.

The small girl rummaged beneath her bin liner and slid a ticket across the desk. Mr Smike inspected it. *Agnethia Toadfax. 13, Coldwinter Street.*

Ridiculous name for a child. But then again, the child was ridiculous, with her tacky home-made costume and overheated imagination.

To his intense disappointment, the ticket seemed to be in order. In stony silence, he stamped the book and pushed it across.

'Right,' he said curtly, pointing to the door. 'No more of your nonsense. Out.'

Agnethia Toadfax opened her mouth, seemed to be about to say something, then closed it again. She picked up her broomstick, tucked her book under her arm and marched out the door without another word.

Mr Smike shook his head and tutted for a considerable length of time.

***

Whatever were parents coming to these days? A good, sharp smack or two, a sight less television and a daily dose of something nasty in a spoon, that's what was needed. With a sniff, he rose, collected his coat and went to turn out the lights.

***

Outside, high above the library roof in the cold October night, Agnethia Toadfax hovered on her broomstick. Her hair streamed out and her binliner cloak flapped madly in the leaf-spinning wind. Below her, the street lamps spilled pools of orange light into the dark, empty street. Up above, wild clouds raced across the full moon.

Should she or shouldn't she? Ma had told her to be careful, to use The Power wisely and not let her temper get the better of her –

but then again, everyone was entitled to a little fun. Especially someone who was just setting out on a Career in Witchcraft. And it *was* Hallowe'en...

'Ah, to heck with it,' she muttered, and twiddled her fingers in a Certain Way. Then, stifling a little giggle, she wheeled her broomstick and headed for home.

It went like the clappers.

***

Behind her and far below, Mr Smike was struggling to turn the key in the lock of the library door.

It was proving a difficult task. Particularly with the thin green webs which had suddenly sprouted between his fingers...

Mbango and the Whirlpool

by Lari Don

Mbango's mother died when she was a baby, so she was brought up by her mother's sister. Her aunt had a daughter of her own, the same age as Mbango, but the aunt didn't treat the two girls equally.

She gave her own daughter all the best food and let her lie around in the sun. She fed Mbango the leftovers and made her do the hardest, nastiest, dirtiest jobs around their hut. If she wasn't satisfied with the work Mbango did, she beat her with a stick.

Mbango's first job every morning was to go to the river to fill the family's calabash with water for cooking and drinking.

One day, Mbango slipped on the mud of the river-bank and dropped the calabash into the water.

The river swept the calabash away. Mbango knew her aunt would beat her if she went home without their only calabash, so she chased it, running along the riverbank, keeping pace with the calabash as the current pulled it along, hoping it would get tangled in weeds or come close enough to the bank for her to reach it.

But it was swept onwards, far out in the speeding river, until Mbango saw a whirlpool ahead. The water was swirling so fast that the centre of the whirlpool was a sharp hole in the river.

The calabash started to spin, sweeping in circles round the edge of the whirlpool, then being pulled nearer the centre. Mbango watched as the calabash was dragged towards the middle, then vanished down the hole and into the depths of the river.

She was more scared of telling her aunt that she had lost their only calabash than she was of the whirlpool. So she closed her eyes, clasped her hands over her head and dived in.

She dived right down to the river bed, and when she opened her eyes she found that she was standing in a village of huts just like her own. She was standing upright, she wasn't wet and she could breathe. But when she looked up, instead of the sky, she saw the whirlpool spinning above her.

When she looked back down she saw the calabash. It had landed on the river bed, and a little old lady had just picked it up.

The little old lady was bent and hunched, with a wrinkled face, bright black eyes and a wide grin showing how few teeth she had left. She was stroking the calabash.

Mbango said to the old lady, 'I'm sorry, but that's my calabash and I dived down here to fetch it.'

'That's a shame,' said the little old lady. 'I don't have a calabash and this is a lovely one.'

Mbango said, 'I am truly sorry, but I do have to take it back to my own village, because if I go home without it my aunt will beat me. Why don't I offer you a fair exchange? I'll do a day's work for you, then you can give me the calabash back.'

So the little old lady took Mbango to her home, a rickety hut at the edge of the village, with a couple of pigs snuffling outside. Mbango spent all day doing the jobs the little old lady was too hunched and weak to do. She fixed the roof and patched the walls, she mucked out the pigs and cleaned the hut inside and out.

When her hut was neat and tidy, the little old lady said, 'I think it's time you went back to your own world and took this calabash to your aunt.'

Mbango sighed and nodded.

'But before you go, I'd be very happy if you'd share a meal with me,' said the little old lady.

So Mbango sat down at the little old lady's table.

Then, with her face shining, her eyes bright and her wide mouth grinning, the little old lady put a plate in front of Mbango. 'Please eat. I hardly ever have guests, and I'd be so honoured if you'd eat with me.'

Mbango looked down.

At a plate of PIG DUNG.

She looked up at the little old lady's eager face and bright eyes.

She looked back down at the plate of pig dung.

Mbango thought, 'I don't want to be rude, I don't want to disappoint or insult this nice old lady, but this is *pig dung*. I can't eat pig dung.'

She looked at the little old lady's happy face and she thought, 'I've done things that are almost as horrid for my aunt and I don't even like her. But I do like this nice old lady and I don't want to offend her.'

So she put her hand out, she picked up the smallest piece of pig dung and she lifted it to her lips...

As she put it to her mouth it turned into a handful of ndole, her favourite fish stew.

Mbango ate everything on the plate and each piece of pig dung turned into wonderful tasty food.

'This is the best meal I've ever had,' she said to the little old lady, who bounced up and down with happiness.

Then the little old lady gave Mbango the calabash and said, 'I have an extra gift for you too, to say thank you for being so helpful and so kind.' She held out three large eggs. 'Break these eggs on the floor of the hut when you get home and they might change your life.'

Mbango said, 'Thank you,' then jumped out of the village, swam up towards the whirlpool, scrambled onto the river bank and ran home to her aunt's hut.

Her aunt picked up a stick and waved it at Mbango. 'Where have you been, you lazy, inconsiderate child?'

Mbango explained, 'I dropped the calabash in the river, then I chased it until it vanished into a whirlpool, so I dived in to get it back. And I found a village under the river and met a little old lady, who gave me back the calabash and these three eggs, and told me to break the eggs on the floor.'

She broke the first egg and out slithered silver chains.

She broke the second egg and out dropped gold nuggets.

She broke the third egg and out tumbled handfuls of diamonds.

The aunt stared at the riches on the floor, then she prodded her own daughter with the stick. 'Go and get us three of those eggs, girl. Go on, now.'

So Mbango's cousin grabbed the calabash and ran to the river. She threw the calabash into the water, she ran along the bank, she saw it vanish into the whirlpool, then she held her nose and jumped in after it.

She found herself in the village, with the whirlpool spinning above. She saw the little old lady stroking the calabash and she yelled, 'Oi! Give that back, it's mine!'

The little old lady handed her the calabash and said, 'Before you go, I'd be honoured if you would join me for a meal.'

'I suppose I'd better,' said Mbango's cousin.

So the little old lady sat her down and offered her a plate of...

'PIG DUNG! You want me to eat pig dung? That's disgusting, you horrible, weird old woman. I'm not eating that!' The cousin stood up, knocking over the table and the plate. 'Just give me my three eggs and I'll be off.'

The little old lady stared at her for a moment, then handed her three eggs. 'I hope you enjoy them.'

Mbango's cousin left the village, swam out of the whirlpool, clambered out of the river, ran home and shouted, 'I got three eggs!'

She smashed the first egg and out slithered snakes.

She threw the second egg against the wall, where it shattered and out dropped scorpions.

She screamed and let go of the third egg, which cracked on the floor and out tumbled spiders.

The snakes and scorpions and spiders chased the aunt and the cousin into the forest. They were never seen again, and that made Mbango's life much happier than any of her new riches. Though she enjoyed the riches too!

Komodo Dragon

by Anita Ganeri

Swinging its head slowly from side to side, a huge, armour-plated creature prowls along a rocky beach. As it wanders along, it flicks its long tongue in and out. It looks as if it has stumbled straight out of the world of the dinosaurs. In fact, this extraordinary reptile is a Komodo dragon, the biggest, heaviest lizard on Earth.

Experts believe that the ancestors of Komodo dragons first lived around 100 million years ago. But it wasn't until the beginning of the 20th century that European scientists were able to confirm that they existed at all.

For hundreds of years, sailors had told stories about real-life, fire-breathing dragons, living on a few tiny islands in Indonesia. They even reported that these dragons could fly. Fascinated by these tales, a Dutch officer, Lieutenant van Steyn van Hensbroek, decided to investigate. A few days after landing on Komodo Island, Indonesia, he shot a dragon and sent the skin to a scientist on the nearby island of Java. The scientist studied it carefully and declared that the animal was a massive monitor lizard. It couldn't fly and it didn't breathe fire, but the dragon name stuck, nevertheless.

News of the discovery spread quickly, and excitement grew. But, so far, the only dragons available to study were dead ones. A live specimen was badly needed. So, in 1926, American naturalist, William

Douglas Burden, headed to Komodo Island to capture a pair of dragons for the Bronx Zoo in New York. Little did he know that his quest for ancient monsters on a mysterious island would inspire the 1933 blockbuster film, *King Kong.*

A Komodo dragon may not actually breathe fire, but it has other horrible hunting habits. Using its tongue to pick up smells from the air, it silently stalks its prey, or waits patiently for it to pass by. Then it launches a deadly attack, killing its victim with a venomous bite. The dragon tears off large chunks of the meat, as big as its head, and swallows them down whole. Nothing is wasted – it happily gobbles down the bones, hooves, skin and insides. In one sitting, a dragon can eat up to three-quarters of its own body weight – that's the same as you devouring around 70 pizzas in one go.

Thanks to their size and fearsome features, Komodo dragons don't have any natural predators. The main threat comes from humans who destroy dragon habitats by logging, clearing land for farming, poaching deer (the dragons' main food) and starting forest fires. Because the dragons are found in so few places, they are very vulnerable if even part of their range is damaged or destroyed. Some dragons may then wander into human territory and prey on livestock, bringing them into conflict with local farmers.

Today, there are around 5,700 wild Komodo dragons, but numbers are falling. To protect them, Komodo National Park was set up in 1980. In 1991, it was declared a UNESCO World Heritage Site. Every year, tens of thousands of tourists visit the park to get a glimpse of its spectacular star attractions. Many local people rely on this tourism to earn a living. Some work as boat drivers or train as wildlife guides. Recently though, a new airport and harbour have brought even more visitors to the islands by plane and cruise ship and it's putting the dragons under serious strain. There are now plans to limit visitor numbers, and to charge an entrance fee, with the money being put towards conservation.

There are also Komodo dragons in zoos around the world. By studying them, and getting to know them better, scientists can help to conserve them in their natural habitat.